ILLUSTRATORS

Patro S. Ulmer, Art Major
Claflin College, Cameron, SC

Brandon McCullough, Art Major
Claflin College, Rock Hill, S.C.

Calonie Johnson, Art Education Major
Claflin College, Santee, SC

Mitchell Waddell, Art Major
Claflin College, Brooklyn, N.Y.

Brandy Nicole Gamble, Art Major
Claflin College, Florence, SC

De Ivory Paige, Art Major
Claflin College, Rock Hill, SC

David Jermaine Moses, Mass
Communications Major
Claflin College, Mayesville, SC

Timothy Dingle, Art Major
Claflin College, St. Stephen, SC

Randy Coard, Art Major
Claflin College, Summerton, SC

Nick Keith, Art Major
Claflin College, Anderson, SC

Damon Johnson, Art Major
Claflin College

Kennetha Bennett, Art Manjor
Claflin College

Corey Epps, Art Major Lake City, SC
Claflin College

Courtney Sims, Claflin College

Toney Brown, Art Major Claflin College

Herman H. Keith, Chairman,
Claflin College Art Dept.

Dominique Lucas, Fourth Grader at
Greenwood Elementary, Florence, SC

Bethune Children Authors of the *Millennium*

Our short stories, fables, poems and illustrations tell the stories of our lives. Hopefully, we will stimulate, excite and inspire you to *"enter the race and cross the finish line"* by sharing your own thoughts and feelings.

We come from all parts of South Carolina and range from second through fifth grades.

Each of us, in our own way, has written a story - a lesson one can learn from - be it good or bad. These stories praise our parents, families, teachers, principals and all others responsible for nurturing and guiding us through the maze of life.

Signed

Anna Marie McCracken	Chelsea Walsh Spencer Blumenberg	Courtney Scott Arlene Perez
Samantha Pedings	Lyndsey Yingst	Renauta Jack
Taylor Hughes	Preston Carwile	Ryan Cooper
Brittany Simmons	Kati Tucker	Isida Konda
Lakeisha Moultrie	Samantha Birch	Charlie Diez
Devarus Moore	Ashley Fain	Nick Meadows
Darius Priester	Brandi Lindsay	Holly Gray
Rashod Helton	Tamieka Gibson	Jamie Chapman
Allysa Woods	Shlanda Edwards	Chelsea Harrell
David Pascutti	Rocky Trammell	Brittany Knox
Cory Jackson	Ciera Jones	Ongela Hill
Deanna Lowe	Seth Rushton	Jordan McKenzie
Mrs. Holladay's 2nd Grade Class	A.J. Lewis' 2nd Graders	Joanna Benjamin's 4th Grade Class
Janet Tillman's 3rd Grade Class	Miss Crumwel's 2nd Grade Class	Mrs. Hankerson's 5th Grade Class

THIS BOOK BELONGS TO

Jereleen Publishing, Inc.
165 West 131st Street, 3Fl.
New York, New York 10027

Web Page: Jereleen.com

email Pub@Jereleen.com

803-534-1992 or 803-453-5482

Copyright © 1999, by Jereleen Publishing, Inc.
Copyright © 1999, illustrations by Jereleen Publishing, Inc.
Computer Graphics and Design by Scott Gandy
Edited by South Carolina Elementary Schools,
Dan Stevenson, and Scott Gandy.

The Bethune Children Authors, 1999
"The Legacy continues to march on"

First Printing 1999

ISBN: 0-9643500-1-7

YOU STARTED OUT AS A SEED
NO ONE KNEW THE COLOR YOU'D BE
THEY WATERED AND NURTURED YOU WELL
AND THEN, ONE DAY,
YOU PIERCED OUT OF YOUR SHELL
THE COLOR OF NIGHT
NO STARS, NO LIGHTS
AN ORIGINAL ROSE
YOU WERE OUT OF SIGHT
PEOPLE WOULD PASS
AND MARVEL
AT YOUR BEAUTY
I'D SIT BACK AND SMILE
HE KNEW THE GLORY
HOWEVER, I KNEW
IT WOULDN'T LAST
YOUR BEAUTIFUL BLACK PETALS
WOULD START TO FALL
YOUR CONFIDENCE WAS SHATTERED
YOU WERE GETTING SMALL
NOW PEOPLE PASSED AND RIDICULED
YOU EVER SO BAD
IN AN EFFORT TO SAVE YOU,
FATE PLAYED THE HAND
I CAN REMEMBER THAT COLD, GLOOMY DAY
AND LIKE THAT BLACK BEAUTIFUL COLOR
I REMEMBERED,
"IT SHINES FOREVER ..."

"The Rose"

By: Telly S.F. Miller

Dedicated To
all the children, parents,
teachers, principals, judges, supporters,
the McLeod family, Bethune family,
and Albert McLeod-Bethune,
grandson and adopted son of
Dr. Mary McLeod Bethune
for making many, many little
dreams come true ...

"The Children Authors"

"BECAUSE OF YOU"

Reading, writing, illustrating, copyrighting, graphics design, promotion and marketing, and yes, publishing, has opened a wider door for children across South Carolina. When we visit our school library or other libraries throughout South Carolina, we can ask for a book written by one or several of our peers. *What a wonderful feeling*, and it's all because of you.

One day soon, we will walk into Books-A-Million, WaldenBooks, Happy Booksellers, R.L. Bryan Bookstore, Barnes and Noble, or a local bookstore, and appreciate even more, why it is so important to read.

When we get on the bus in the morning, we are eager to go to school to learn even more about reading, writing and publishing.

Guess what? *"It's all because of you."*

Rep. John L. Scott, Jr.,
Sen. John C. Land, III,
And
Eddie L. Miller, Jr., Publisher

Sincerely,

Dr. Bethune Children Authors

Dr. Bethune
Children Authors
1999

Table of Contents

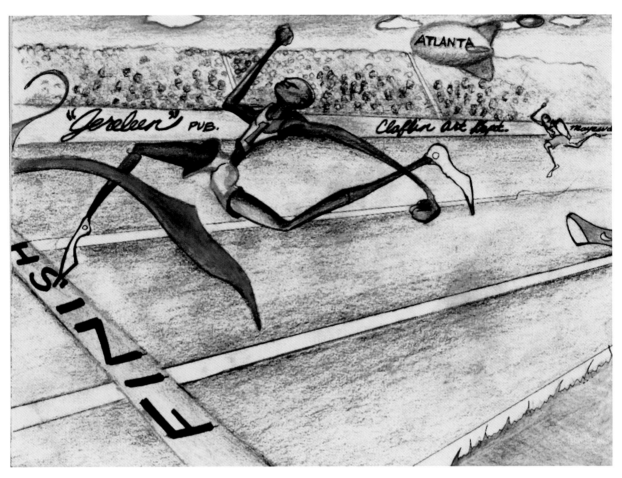

CURTIS RACES IN THE RACE

By Rashod Helton

Curtis is tall, handsome and smart. One day he saw a poster hanging on the wall beside the gym door. He could hear Coach Kirby telling the other students what to do. He read what the poster said, "If you want to try out for the Olympic team in Atlanta, come to the track after school." He knew he would be there because he was the best runner ever and could beat anyone in a race. That's why the girls were all over him.

Curtis was so excited when he began to read the poster, he read some more. It said, "We will pick one person for the tryouts." Curtis knew he was going to win this race. On the way to his locker, Curtis gave everyone a high five. After he got his stuff out of his locker, he went to class. Curtis never felt this happy before.

While he was in school he kept a smile on his face. He just couldn't forget the moment when he read that poster in the crowded and noisy hall. He thought that was the best thing that could ever happen to him. All Curtis kept on his mind was the race. After his warm up, he went over to the coaches and students. Coach Conners, the gym coach, was at the starting line and Coach Kirby was at the finish line.

Coach Conners yelled, *"On Your Mark, Get Set, Go!"* Curtis was the first person out of the starting blocks. When he was running he turned his head to see where everyone was. They were way behind him. Curtis won the race in record time. He was so happy. Coach Kirby walked him back to the starting line where Coach Conners was. They were impressed with his time. Coach Kirby told Curtis he would come by his house and give his parents a list of things he would need for his trip to the Olympic tryouts in Atlanta. Curtis was so happy, he ran all the way home. When he got home he told his parents the good news. "This calls for a celebration," said Curtis' father excitedly. Curtis chose the restaurant that he wanted to go to, because it had the best food in town and did not cost a whole lot.

Coach Kirby came to the house later that night. He told Curtis parents all about how Curtis had won the race at school. Coach Kirby gave Curtis' mom the information needed for the trip to Atlanta. Curtis' mom and dad just could not believe what they heard. He woke up the next morning talking about the race, even as they packed, he talked more.

Curtis and his parents arrived at the airport at 8:30 a.m. As they boarded the plane, the flight attendant took them to the First Class Section. There was a lot of noise because of people holding conversations with each other. Curtis put on his headphones, turned his radio on, and looked out the window. All he saw was the sky with white clouds.

The airplane ride lasted for an hour, and they watched a real good movie. The movie was about two men that saved a girl from being killed. When Curtis and his parents arrived in Atlanta, the Olympic coach was already there to greet them. The coach introduced himself as Coach Parker. Curtis introduced himself, his mom and dad. Afterwards, they caught a bus going to 100 Washington St.

When they got off the bus, the first thing Curtis did was to look at the name of the place. It was the *Olympic Tryout Academy*. After they looked around the academy, they went to the Old Harriot Hotel. Curtis had his very own room. After Curtis and his parents finished unpacking, they went back to the Academy. Coach Parker showed them around some more.

Afterwards, they went outside and looked at the stadium. The track had lanes drawn on it. The Academy was the best place Curtis had ever seen. Coach Parker explained that the race would be in two days. During those two days, Curtis did things to build up his strength for the race. He went to the gym in Atlanta and worked out for 4 hours.

Finally, the big day arrived. Curtis was up at 6:00 a.m.. He was tense and too excited to relax, so he went for a walk to calm down. After Curtis returned to the hotel, he washed, dressed and packed his running gear. When Curtis was leaving the hotel, he saw Coach Parker who had been looking for him. He handed Curtis a list of the boys that were also trying out for the team. Curtis knew that he had to beat those boys. When he looked at the list, there were ten names. There was a Michael Hudson, Daryl Holmes, Mike Mitchell, Parker Stanton, Peter Parker, Mark Carey, Spike Silver, Christopher Owens, Matthew Conners, and Carl Cooper.

Coach Parker told Curtis that the boys were mighty fast, but that he didn't have anything to worry about. "Come with me," he said. "I want to show you how they look."

They went to Bultman Drive and pulled up to a place called Championship Leaders. The music was blasting and could be heard outside. Curtis and Coach Parker got out of the car and went to the door. Coach Parker opened the door and the music was even louder. Coach Parker turned down the radio and went into another room. He told Curtis to follow him, and in the room, some boys were shooting darts and they looked really strong. The boys were talking about how they were going to win the race. They talked about what they would do in the Olympics. Curtis just could not take it anymore, so he left.

Coach Parker and Curtis went to the Academy. It was time for the race. The people started to fill the stands and by 2:43 p.m., the stands were filled. Then the boys arrived. Each boy, including Curtis, lined up on the track. Coach Parker said, "Good Luck." And then, *"On Your Mark, Get Set ..."* the gun went off and Curtis was off and running. The other boys were way behind. He crossed the finish line in a matter of seconds. He won the race. He was now a member of the *U.S. Olympic Team*.

A
CHILD'S
STRUGGLE

Written by:
Cory Jackson

Illustrated by:
Dominique Lucas

School Is Cool !

Mya had hoped that she had made a 100% on her spelling test. She had been making bad grades for the last few weeks. Her mother said she had to improve her grades or else something was going to happen that she didn't want to happen.

The teacher, Mrs. Patterson, called out names to come get their spelling papers. She asked Jack, Karen, Susan, and Mya to please come and get their papers.

Karen and Mya looked at each other. They were best friends. Karen had helped Mya study for her spelling test. Actually, they played around instead of studying. Karen smiled at Mya, but Mya frowned back at Karen. Mrs. Patterson called Mya and a girl named Sharon to her desk.

    She said, "The grades I've been seeing from you two have been really bad. I'd like you two to improve these grades."

    "Yes, Mrs. Patterson." They both replied quickly.

    Mrs. Patterson said, "You may take your seat now." Mya walked quickly back to her desk and stared at the big red F on her spelling paper. She was so disappointed!

Walking home from school, Karen asked Mya how she did on her spelling test.

"Uh...Uh...I made a B+," she replied with a guilty expression on her face.

Karen said, "That is great!" Then she asked Mya to come to her house after school.

"Sorry Karen, but I'm on restriction for not cleaning my room." "Okay, see you later then!" Karen said as she came to her block.

　　As Mya walked she thought about how she was going to tell her mother that she made an F on her spelling test. She had promised her mother that she would improve her spelling grade. She decided that she would get her mother to sign her paper at the last minute.

The next morning, Mya asked her mother to sign the spelling paper. She covered the red F on her paper. Her mother asked what it was.

"Oh nothing but a paper about the APT meeting this Monday night," answered Mya.

"If you will move your hand, maybe I can sign it, Mya," Mya's mother said.

Mya moved her hand and her mother saw the red F on Mya's paper.

 Mya wanted to burst into tears right then, and she did.

 Her mother said, "Come straight home after school and we will talk. Hurry up before the bus leaves you!"

 When Mya got on the bus, she sat beside Karen. She felt guilty after telling her best friend a big lie. She knew that Karen would never forgive her.

Mya and Karen went in the room quickly and sat down. Mrs. Patterson called out names for signed papers. "Mya, bring me your signed papers," said Mrs. Patterson. "I'd like to see the spelling sheet first, please." Mya showed her the spelling paper. Mrs. Patterson just stared. Mrs. Patterson told Mya that she could have a seat now.

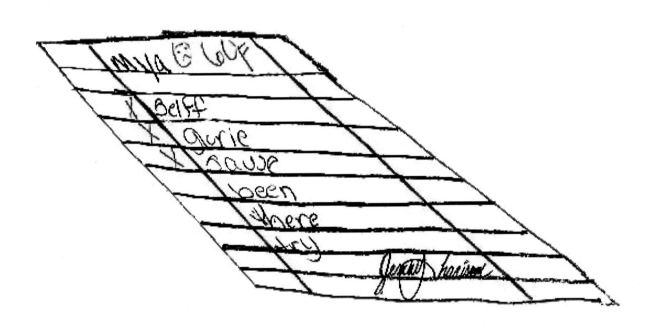

Mya walked quickly back to her seat. Karen winked at Mya. When Mya got home from school, she went straight to her room. She took out her spelling notebook. Mya studied and studied until she fell asleep.

Early the next morning, Mya woke up lying in the bed with her pajamas on. She hadn't remembered putting on her pajamas last night. Her mother must have put them on her. Mya looked at her alarm clock and it was 2:30 a.m. Mya tried to go back to sleep, and finally she did.

14

Mya had a dream that she made an A+ on her next spelling test. She kept saying, "Yes! Yes!" Mya woke up saying, "Yes! Yes!"

Her mother was shaking her and telling her to wake up. They had overslept! It was 7:30 a.m.

When Mya got to school, the class was taking the spelling test. Mya thought to herself that she had come at a bad time. The teacher told her to number her paper from one through ten and start at number three. Mrs. Patterson said she would go back and call out the rest of the words when they finished.

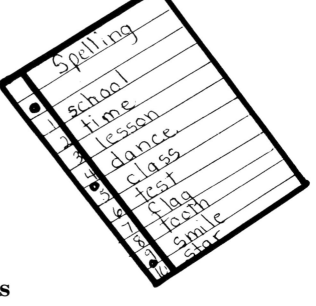

This is how Mya's paper looked when she finished with this week's test.

The teacher gave her back her paper from the day before. Mya saw a black A+ on it! She jumped up and screamed, "Yes!" Mya felt proud of herself. She had learned a very valuable lesson. She would always study for her tests. It is better to be prepared than to worry. On the way home, Mya explained to Karen about the lie, and Karen accepted her apology. Mya was happy again. She just couldn't wait to tell her mom the good news!

Susie and The Great BIG FIRE

By Mrs. Holladay's Language Arts Class

Once there was a match named Smokey. All day long, Smokey sat in a dark, cold, lonely matchbox.

One day, a girl named Susie took him
out of the box to play with him.

What she didn't know, were the dangers
that were waiting ahead for her.

Susie was a very curious little girl.

She picked up Smokey and started to throw him up and catch him.

Then, she began to wonder about the box Smokey was in.

She had seen her dad strike matches on the box before so she decided she would try it.

Suddenly, Smokey burst into flames!

As the flames grew bigger, she became nervous, and somehow the match tumbled to the floor.

A few seconds later, her parents bedroom was on fire. Susie was scared because she didn't know what to do.

Then, she remembered about a year ago, her mother telling her what to do in case of a fire. She had said, "In case of a fire, find the nearest way out, window or door. Meet everyone else at the clothes line, our meeting place."

Susie ran out of the house and to the clothes line. When she got there, she was very happy to find her parents there. They each gave her a big hug. Then she noticed her big brother was missing. She immediately asked where he was. As she heard the sirens blowing in the background, her brother was running back from their neighbor's house. He had called 911.

Susie had learned her lesson.

She would never play with matches again.

SHE DIDN'T!

Fire Safety Check List

Things To Have

Smoke detector

Fire extinguisher

Designated meeting place

Things To Do

Crawl low under the smoke.

Meet at a designated meeting place.

Never return to a burning building.

Feel closed doors with the back of your hand, if hot, use another exit.

THE PRETTY Rainbow

By Brittany Simmons

Once there was a little girl. Her name was Nicole.

Her father usually took her different places. On this one particular day, her father woke her up early. She asked her father, "But, why do I have to get up so early?" Her father said, "Because we're going camping!"

Then she said, "Okay." She was so happy; she rushed and got dressed. After she got dressed, Nicole began helping her father pack everything that was needed for the trip. After all the packing was finished, they finally left to go camping.

On the way to the camp site, Nicole was daydreaming about a pretty rainbow with lots of butterflies and flowers around it.

Finally, they arrived at the campsite. Nicole said to her father, "This looks like a good place to set up our tent."

Her father said, "That is a perfect place for our tent." When Nicole's father was finished setting up the tent, she asked him, "How long are we going to be here, Daddy?"

He said, "One week."

Soon, one day had gone by. Then, the second day... and on the third day, Nicole and her father jumped rope, played games, and sang some of their favorite songs.

Nicole was having so much fun. All of a sudden, she envisioned a pretty rainbow and started to smile. Her father said, "Tomorrow, we'll go do a little exploring." She replied, "That will be nice."

Soon, morning came. It was time to get up. Nicole was ready to explore the woods. She was hoping she would get to see a pretty rainbow again.

As she and her father walked through the woods, they ran across squirrels, rabbits, butterflies, and even a pond with lots of frogs, but she didn't see a pretty rainbow.

The last day of the camping trip, her father decided to take her fishing. They walked across two hills to get to the fishing pond.

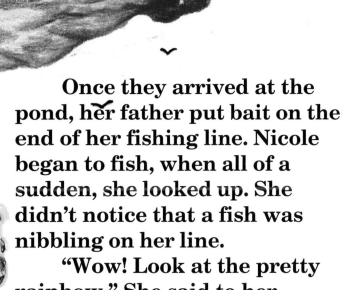

Once they arrived at the pond, her father put bait on the end of her fishing line. Nicole began to fish, when all of a sudden, she looked up. She didn't notice that a fish was nibbling on her line.

"Wow! Look at the pretty rainbow." She said to her father, "That's the prettiest rainbow I have ever seen." Nicole was *not* upset about not catching any fish.

When I Grow Up
By Darius Priester

I like to play football very much.
When I grow up I want to be a
famous football player.

I'll do my best to be a good player. I will get paid lots of money and I will not miss a game.

I'll kick the ball so hard, it will soar high over the goal post. If I don't make the field goal, that'll be all right because I'll stop the other team from getting the ball. I'll tackle the player down to the ground. And, if I get the fumbled ball, I'll run as fast as I can to make a touch down.

I like nice people. I hope my coach is nice, and even if he is not nice, I'll be nice to him.

If, I am the quarterback, I'll throw the ball to a team member. I hope he catches it and runs for a touch down.

Maybe, I'll be a superstar. If someone sees me, and asks me for my autograph, I'll give it to them. And, if it's a boy, I'll ask, "Do you want to be a famous football player, also?"

I'll finish college . I will retire at age 40. My fans will admire me. I will be rich. I will buy my family nice things.

"STEVE"
By David Pascutti

Dinosaurs lived long ago, but we can still learn about them today.

People called "Paleontologists" find their remains. Paleontologists do not find dinosaurs, but find their bones, teeth, and eggs. These are called "fossils." Paleontologists also find fossils of plants and other animals that lived long ago.

There was a young boy named "Steve." He couldn't wait to grow up to become a Paleontologist.

Steve's father was also a Paleontologist. Their house was just like a museum. Almost everywhere you looked were bones, fossils, and teeth.

One night, when Steve was asleep, he had a dream that he was on a fossil hunt with his father. He found an egg worth a million dollars.

The next morning, Steve convinced his father to take him on a fossil hunt. He was determined to find something.

All day, Steve searched high and low for the priceless egg. He didn't find the million-dollar egg, but he did find a dinosaur bone.

Even though Steve did not find the million-dollar egg, he was still happy. Young Steve's bone was displayed in a museum. The curator of the museum put up a sign that said, "Found by Steve, a young Paleontologist."

If you want to be a Paleontologist when you grow up, maybe you could ask your father to take you on a fossil hunt. Who knows what you might find? Maybe, you just might become a "young Paleontologist" like Steve!

The Mice Are in the Rice

By Miss Crumel's Class

Diesha Berry

Jolena Branch

Rakam Davis

Christopher Felder

Audreanna Fogle

Charles Harrison

Sheldon Johnson

Olandria Jones

Lee Mack

Latavia Mack

Queen Mack

Austin Morris

Adrienne Myers

James Meyers

Destiny Roberts

Xavier Shuler

Porsche Stokes

Ryan Valentine

Niasha Williams

Olandria woke up and
began to shout,

"The mice are in the rice and they won't get out!"

Olandria told Latavia
and she began to shout,

"The snakes are in the lake and they won't get out!"

Latavia told Niasha and
she began to shout,

"The fleas are in the peas and they won't get out!"

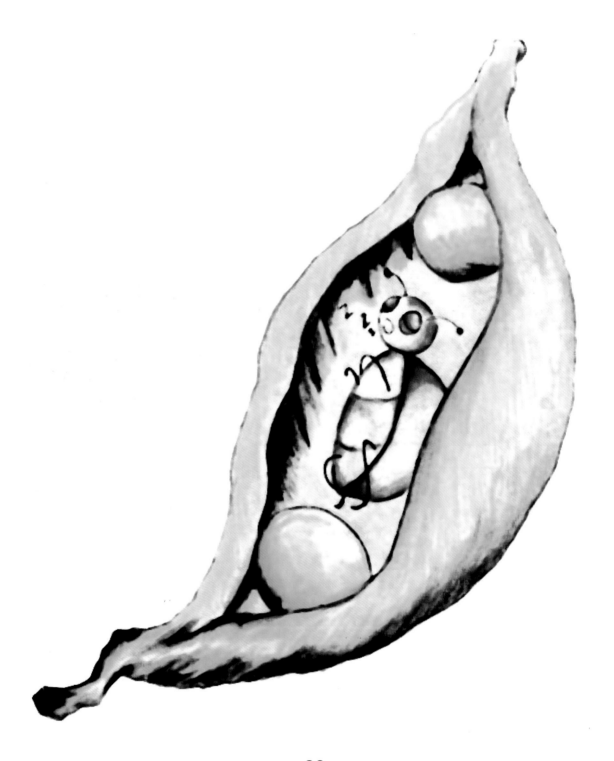

Niasha told Xavier and
he began to shout,

"The bees are in the trees and they won't get out!"

Xavier told Diesha and she didn't budge. She didn't laugh and she didn't nudge.

She grabbed her great, big stick and she said,

"I bet I'll make you move real quick!"

42

Who Knows What Milly Tilly Is Going to Do Next?

By
Tamieka
Gibson

Once upon a time there was a guard dog named Silly Billy. There was also a cat named Hilly Zilly and a rat named Milly Tilly, who was a thief.

43

One night, Willy Dilly and his mother had dinner. Milly Tilly came in and stole a piece of meat from the plate. Silly Billy was about to jump on her, but Hilly Zilly saved her. Silly Billy jumped on the table, and Willy Dilly put him outside. He looked for Milly Tilly, but she was already in her hole.

When Silly Billy went into his little house, Milly Tilly came back out and ate the rest of the meat she left out. She could not bite into it. Do you know why? Since Milly Tilly couldn't bite it she swallowed it, and something happened. When morning came, Willy Dilly untied Silly Billy. Everything was very still.

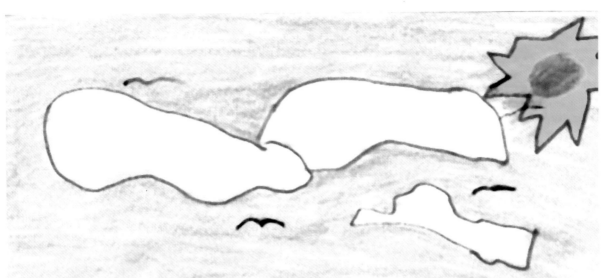

Years later Milly Tilly woke up. She felt something funny. She saw her legs come back and felt her teeth coming through her gums.

Silly Billy never messed with Milly Tilly gain.

Moral

Never eat something if you don't know what it is!!!

The Two Dinosaurs
By Lakeisha Moultrie

One day, I met two dinosaurs walking down the street. They were so tall that they could look in your house.

I was walking down the street and I met Big Ben, the dinosaur, and we went to the park and played and talked.

Then I went home and Diamond Cliff, the dinosaur, came walking down the street. He knocked on my door. I let him in and we started to talk. He asked if he could be a part of our family. "Yes, you may, Cliff."

My mom, dad, and I said that you could be a part of my family. Big Ben got jealous, so he moved in with us, too. The three of us played together every day at the park.

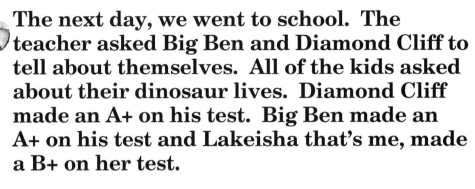

The next day, we went to school. The teacher asked Big Ben and Diamond Cliff to tell about themselves. All of the kids asked about their dinosaur lives. Diamond Cliff made an A+ on his test. Big Ben made an A+ on his test and Lakeisha that's me, made a B+ on her test.

After school, my mother cooked a big pot of spaghetti. It was so good, she had to cook another pot. It was too good! Diamond Cliff and Big Ben had it on their mouths and their fingers. After we ate, we took a good hot bath and went to sleep.

When I woke up, everyone was out of their rooms and downstairs. I realized that it was my birthday. My mom had boiled some eggs and cooked grits and bacon. My brother had poured the orange juice. We took a wash-up and went to school.

We went to lunch. At lunch, Diamond Cliff bumped his head on the wooden door. His diamond earring fell on the floor. Big Ben asked Lakeisha to crawl under the table to get the diamond earring. Lakeisha, that's me, the shortest girl in school, crawled under the tiny table and got the diamond earring.

We went home and played outside all day long. When I got inside, my dad said, "SURPRISE! Happy Birthday!" I told my dad that it is okay to help someone in need.

We ate and went to bed!

What Makes Crestview A Great School?
By: Taylor Hughes

Crestview is a great school because we have nice teachers, terrific students, and a super principal. The teachers always let us do fun things, not boring things. We also have friendly students that play together at recess. Our principal is nice too. She always waves or says hello to us in the hall.

We have a neat playground. There are lots of hiding places and wide spaces to run and play. We also have a fossil dig on the playground with shark teeth and stingray blades. It has many shells too.

We have some neat programs at Crestview like the PE Club, Chorus, Sideways Storytellers, Library Helpers, Student Council, and Art Club. We have to try out to get in to Chorus. Once you are in, you sing after school one or two days a week. In Sideways Storytellers, you read, write, tell stories, and act out stories for the kindergartners and other people. In Art Club, you draw, paint and sometimes you do crayon sketches.

The PTA does great things for everybody in the school. They plan really neat assemblies for us. At the Ronald McDonald assembly they gave away Tamagotchies and cups. We have volunteers that copy worksheets for the teachers and plan parties for us. In our class, the room mother and teacher planned a fruit tasting party. We got to taste different kinds of fruit. Parents really help to make our school great.

Our related arts classes make Crestview exciting because they are fun. When we go to PE, we play lots of fun games that help develop our muscles. In Art, we draw, paint, and talk about artists. In Guidance, Mrs. Tyler, our guidance counselor, plays with us too. In Music, we sing and play instruments.

So you see, Crestview is really a wonderful school. We have a great staff, and we have fun learning.

Crestview is Great
By: Jennifer Fuller

I know Crestview is the greatest school because I go there. Just think about how long Crestview has been around. My mom went to Crestview and she loved Crestview just like I do.

Without the teachers, principals, faculty, and volunteers, Crestview wouldn't be a great school. All these people work hard everyday to make our school better. No other school is like Crestview. Crestview has a great PTA, one that cares. Crestview also has a wonderful principal. Our principal, Mrs. Thomason, cares about the school and the students. She wants our school to improve in every way possible. Crestview is very fortunate to have a science lab and a gym. Did you know that only four elementary schools in Greenville County have a science lab? That is also true about the gym.

We are very lucky to have a brand new school building. Crestview has clean and quiet halls. Crestview also has a clean lunchroom. We have fresh food everyday with a variety of choices. Inside our classrooms, we have white boards instead of chalkboards. White boards are better because if you use a chalkboard you will get chalk dust all over your hands and you will have to beat the erasers. We are lucky to have after school clubs and dances. We have clubs such as PE, Art, and Chorus.

If I had a choice of any school in the world, I would choose Crestview! Thank you Crestview for everything! These are only a few reasons, out of a thousand, why Crestview is great!

THE CIRCUS IS COMING

By A.J. Lewis Greenview's
2nd Grade Class

Spring was in full bloom. The birds were happy - chirping from tree to tree. Bees were buzzing about and even Miss Grumpy Tussy, the class rabbit, appeared to be happy.

Happiness was running wild everywhere - except with the children in Miss A.J. Lewis' second grade class. Their faces were long and down to their feet. Their spirits were down in the mud. They were just plumb tired and drained from burying their heads in books all year long. Now, they were bored silly and did not have anything exciting to do for the Spring.

They didn't complain, but they walked around miserable and sad all day.

It was near the end of the school day, when Mrs. Packson, the Music teacher, and Miss Huckson, the Art teacher, could not take another moment of seeing all those sad faces dragging around the school.

They put their heads together and came up with the most brilliant idea ever. They would have the students put on a production.

"This will definitely replace every frown with a smile," explained Mrs. Packson.

"Well, now let's see," said Miss Huckson. "What can the students do?"

After thinking about it for a moment, Miss Huckson shouted excitingly. "I think I've got it! Since the second graders have been learning about different animals, it would be just perfect for them to put on a circus production."

51

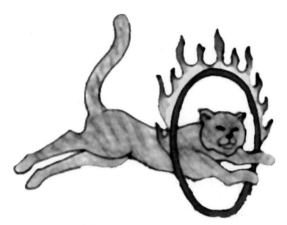

"Yes, that would definitely work!" said Miss Huckson. "I know the kindergartners would jump at the idea of doing the alphabet. Since the first graders enjoyed the movie 'Aladdin' at the theater the other day, a magic carpet production for them will be perfect.

"Ah, now, our third graders," Miss Huckson sighed. "It won't be easy brewing up magic for them."

Again, the two teachers put their heads together, and suddenly, Mrs. Packson shouted out excitedly, "A Musical Nutcracker! That would be great fun for the third graders!"

"The fourth graders will do United States History. For the fifth graders, nothing less than their best, an original opera!"

"Terrific! That's what we'll do!" they both shouted.

It was now settled.

Both Mrs. Packson and Miss Huckson attended training at a special school out west for this very thing. So putting on a school production would be an easy task for them. They shared all the new things they had learned about production with the students, as they planned for the circus.

Every student was excited. They began to practice and learn their different parts. They practiced and practiced everyday until it was time to perform the production.

The morning of the circus production, the children were ecstatic as they jumped off the buses. Their faces were glowing and screams of excitement were heard all over the school. Tired and bored had not been seen since all of this got started. The children were happy again and doing what they liked.

The day got started out beautifully. The skies were clear and the sun was shining brightly. It was hot. Everything was perfect. Joy, laughter, and excitement filled the school as Mrs. Milliard, the principal, moved the children rapidly to their classrooms.

"Today is the big day!" cried Mrs. Milliard. "Everyone is eager to see this big production!"

The children had to rush to their classes and get into their costumes. While some were busy yanking, pulling, and tugging, the others were frantically humming the songs they had practiced.

Meanwhile, Mrs. Milliard was sitting at the desk in her office, when a disturbing news announcement was heard on her radio. All she heard was.

"Tornado!" shouted Mrs. Milliard. "It can't be!" Then she moved closer to the radio and listened very carefully.

The man cried out again, "Tornado sighting 10 miles west of Columbia!"

"Oh, my goodness!" cried Mrs. Milliard. "I must hurry and warn everyone."

"Uh Um," she said into the intercom as she cleared her throat. "Teachers and students, all school year we have practiced tornado drills. Now I want to see how everyone can follow those same procedures. Now, move quickly."

The children listened quietly and did everything the teachers told them to do. A frightened look came over the little faces of every child in the room.

While the teachers appeared to be as cool as cucumbers, they were shaking down to their knees!

Just before they could think about what was going to happen with the production, Mrs. Milliard received the best news yet.

The tornado that was sighted was no longer a threat.

Smiles were once again on their faces. Tired and bored silly never ever came back again.

The ring master yelled into his bull horn, "Ladies and gents ... boys and girls! Let the circus begin!"

Applause. Applause. Excitement filled the air.

"RRRRRR!" roared the lions. "Tut, tut, tut!" blew the elephants as they trampled and stumped clumsily all around. The tightrope dancers performed cute somersaults on the skimpiest wire over our heads.

It was a great day! A great day all around.

My Runaway Imagination

By Ms. Benjamin's 4th Grade Class

IMAGINATION HAS ENDLESS POSSIBILITIES ...

Imagination is a clever thing; it allows the mind to grow. What if backpacks could talk? If you lose your homework, it would tell you where to go.

You could become anything you wanted, like a magical wizard or a super human who could lift two thousand tons.

My-My that
imagination could
take you away ...
Fly to an invisible
castle, no one has
ever visited
before.

On the other hand ...

Imagination could be
a terrible thing when
the wrong person
opens a door.

If bats grew to be 100 feet long and 50 feet wide, the world would become a scary place.

What would happen if my teacher gave quizzes everyday and knots grew on my face?

How would we feel if cows ate us instead of us eating them?

What if parents knew our every move through an ongoing action film?

The world would be
a lonely place if we
did not have
imagination!
Imagination is a
clever thing; it allows
the mind to grow...

It's like the old
saying, "The more you
grow, the more you
need to know!"

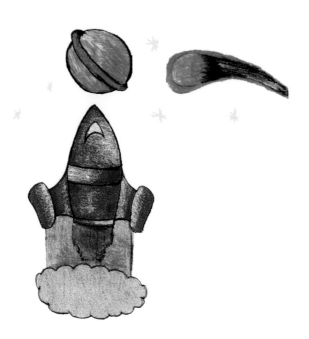

I am imagining
a special
kidcraft that
travels to a
different place.
On each craft
are kids from
each galaxy
and race.

I am imagining many things,
now it is your turn.

Take my place.

Imagination is a clever thing, so use it!

I did ...

There's a Dinosaur In My Science Class!

By Samantha G. Pedings

Have you ever wondered why the dinosaurs died? There are many theories about why they died. Do you think they could have done something to keep from being extinct? I think that if they went to school, the dinosaurs still would be alive today.

One of the theories of why dinosaurs died is that the climate got too cold for them to survive. If they had been taught geography, they could have moved closer to the equator where it is warmer.

Or if they had taken a course called Home Economics, they could have learned to sew warm clothes.

Another theory is that new plants started growing, and the dinosaurs couldn't eat them. If they had taken Home Economics, they could have learned a way to cook them so they could eat them.

Another theory is that meteors hit the earth, and dust formed and blocked out the sunlight. If the dinosaurs had read a science book, they might have figured out how to make big vacuums to clean up all of the dust and dirt out of the air.

Also in science, they might have learned how to make radar machines to see if another meteor was coming towards earth.

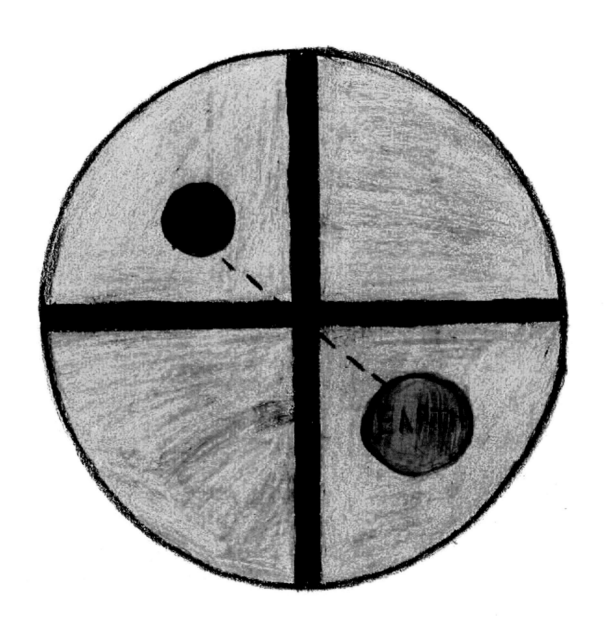

The next time you think you don't need an education, think about how the dinosaurs might be alive today if they went to school.

YOU NEVER KNOW WHAT TOMORROW WILL BRING, AND AN EDUCATION WILL PREPARE YOU FOR THE CHALLENGES OF THE FUTURE.

THE COPYCAT WHO THOUGHT SHE WAS SMART

By: Brittany Knox

Yesterday, a new girl named Melenie came to our class. She said, she was smart and knew everything that she needed to know.

When we took our multiplication test, I saw the new girl looking on Suzana's paper.

Later, Mrs. Magical called Melenie and Suzana to her desk. "Well girls," she said. "We have a problem. Your papers look the same and the only thing I can see is that, Suzana, you haven't been doing well on your multiplication lately, and Melenie said she is smart. It leads me to believe Melenie."

When it was lunchtime, I sat beside Melenie. "Look!" I said. "I know you cheated, but I didn't say anything. You have to tell Mrs. Magical the truth."

Melenie stared straight into my eyes and said, "Looka here Bucko! You better not open your mouth and tell a soul or else!"

She threatened me. I could not believe it. I thought she was nice. But, she is a mean and ugly person.

After lunch, we went back to class. We had to take a spelling test.

Mrs. Magical said, "Okay class, the first word is minerals." I looked up and saw Melenie cheating, again. Mrs. Magical saw her too.

She called Melenie to her desk and said, "I'm happy and sad. Happy to have learned the truth and sad to find out that you couldn't tell the truth." Melenie tried to deny it at first, but Mrs. Magical said, "I saw you looking on Suzana's paper. You will take both tests over. Class dismissed."

Melenie cried and stared at me as I was leaving. Mrs. Magical had given Melenie a second chance because she was new. But, she was never to do that again.

I wanted to tease and call her, "The copycat who thought she was smart," but that wouldn't have solved anything.

The Missing Robber
By Steven Cheyney

Once upon a time, there was a pig who had a Harley and he went to the store to go shopping.

When he got there, there was a robber robbing Mal-Mart.

The robber saw the pig, but the robber got all of the money and left. The pig got on his Harley and took out after him!

The cops stopped the robber
and got all the money. They took
the robber to jail.
   The pig got a 2,000 dollar
reward because the cops were
hunting the robber for two years.

The pig bought himself a new
house with lots of food and a T.V.
He lived happily ever after!

THE DAY KATHRYN'S CAT TAUGHT THE CLASS

By Kati Tucker

"Well, how was your day dear?" asked Sydney's mom.
"Oh, kind of dull, until Mrs. Kitty came in the room,"
answered Sydney.
"Mrs. Kitty? What kind of name is that for a teacher?"
"Well, it would be a good name for a teacher who is a
cat!"
"Your teacher was a cat?"
"Yes ma'am. My teacher was a cat!"
"What was a cat doing at school?"

"Kathryn wanted her cat to meet the class! When the principal heard this, she loved the idea and the cat became our teacher."

"First, we had to show Mrs. Kitty how to teach a room full of kids. Then, Kathryn promised to help Mrs. Kitty every night."

"What does your class have for homework?"

"No one in our class has homework except Kathryn because she had to help Mrs. Kitty."

"We'll have Mrs. Kitty as our teacher for two weeks!"

"Is she nice to your classmates and you?"

"Yes, she is very nice to all of us! We all love Mrs. Kitty a lot! She let us have a party and it's only Monday."

"Well, Sydney, it sounds like you have had a good day."

"Yes mom, we had a great time today with Mrs. Kitty."

Wagon Of Dreams

By Samantha Birch

My teacher has just asked me to write about what I would put in my "wagon of dreams." In my wagon of dreams I would have plenty of things and these are a few of them.

In my wagon, the first thing I would have would be God. When I grow up, I want to be the President of the United States of America. That has been my goal for a long time. To be a woman President would be hard. Many have tried, but none have succeeded. If I want to be President, many people will laugh and give up on me, but the person that will be there, the whole way, is God.

The next thing I would have in my wagon would be my friends. I want my friends to be there for me when I need a shoulder to cry on. I would need their love and support.

I would also need in my wagon, strength and faith in myself and, with that, I would need determination and confidence.

Also, I would need my family. I would need my family's love, support, and money. They would be the people I would fall back on.

I would need education in my wagon. I would need it so that I can be someone in my life. I can not fail in school and become President. If I am going to be President, it would be best to go to law school. I will need to study hard and make good grades.

While I am in office, I will be making many important decisions. I will have to make good choices for our country. I will also have to care about our country and the needs of the people in it.

After I am President, I want people to look back and remember me as the first female President of the United States of America.

My wagon is filled with dreams. I just have to be careful that it does not tip over.

Monkey's Visit to the Banana Shack
By Rocky Trammell

Once upon a time, a monkey named Tom was walking to a tree to play, but on the way, he saw a sign that said, "Banana Shack." The sign said to turn right. So he went that way and he saw a door. He opened it. Inside, he saw bananas all over the shack.

He went "BANANAS" and ate them ALL!

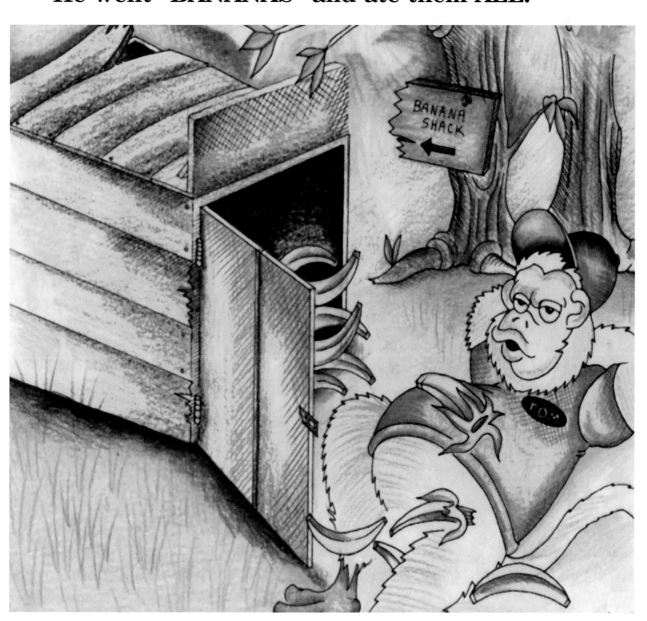

Mathew's Tooth

By Ashley Fain

Mathew had a loose tooth. One morning, Mathew got out of bed, got dressed, and went downstairs. He ate his breakfast. Then he said his tooth hurt.

His mom looked in his mouth. She said he had a loose tooth. He said he knew that. Then he finished his breakfast and went to school. At twelve o'clock he ate lunch. He bit into his apple.

He told his teacher that his tooth was hurting. She sent him to the school nurse. She said he had a loose tooth. He said he knew that.

When he got home he went to the bathroom and tried to pull his tooth, but it would not come out. His mom called "Dinner's ready!" so he went downstairs to eat his supper. When he finished his supper, he noticed his tooth was gone.

He went looking for his tooth. He found his tooth under his chair. His mother said, "When you go to sleep, put it under your pillow." When Mathew heard those words he was so excited. He wanted to go to sleep right then, but his Mother said, "You have to do your homework, take your bath, and then you can go to sleep."

So he finished his homework. Then he took his bath. He put on his pajamas and hopped into bed. He put his tooth under his pillow. He fell asleep.

Then the Tooth Fairy came in. She knocked over everything. She made so much noise she woke up Mathew. Mathew saw the Tooth Fairy. He was amazed. He gave her his tooth. She gave him a quarter. He said his name was Mathew. She said her name was Tooth Fairy. They were friends from that day on.

Seven Little Bees

By Brandi Lindsay

Once there were seven little bees. Their names were Buzzy, John, Mary, Fuzzy, Dorothy, Lucy, and Sally. They all lived with their mother and father in a round beehive. Their mother's name was Lucille and their father's name was McDuff.

One sunny day, they all went out to play. While they were playing, dragonflies began to chase them. They flew as fast as they could past a bunch of trees to escape. All except Fuzzy, who bumped into a tree. He bumped the tree so hard, that it made him silly. He yelled for his brothers and sisters to help him. All at once, all of the bees began to chase the dragonflies until the dragonflies were out of sight.

Feeling so brave, the bees returned home at last.

A Story of Love
By Anna Marie McCracken

Once upon a time, there lived an old woman that lived miles away from this old man who had problems with his heart. But every day he acted like he was feeling very good at home.

This old man's name was Frankie Handcock. He always said, "I will never die." He always came over to that old woman's house. "Will you feed me?" he always asked. The old woman knew that he wanted to marry her, so they married, but after their marriage, the old man died.

The woman would always love him. The doctor tried to get his heart to beat again, but it was too late. The old man died from a heart attack.

The Story of the Woods
By Shlanda Edwards

One day I was walking in the woods. It was dark and I was scared. I was scared because I heard a snake making this loud noise. I didn't know what to do, so I didn't move or say anything. When the snake left I got up and ran. It was getting darker. After I ran a little while I saw this house, so I went in. There was this old lady in there and I said, "Excuse me." She turned around. I looked at her very close. It was my grandmother, Sherrie. I ran and gave her a hug. She didn't know what to do.

I said, "Grandma, I saw a snake and it scared me!"

She asked, "Keosha, What else did you see?"

I said, "I saw this old house. I was scared to come in here. I thought this was just a rusty, old house. So I walked in and I saw you. Grandma, I am hungry, so hungry - very, very, very hungry!"

"What do you want to eat?" Grandma asked.

"Some good old beans and some corn bread! What do you want to do after we finish eating?" Keosha asked.

"I want to go to sleep next," said Grandma.

"I am getting sleepy right now," said the little girl.

So, sleep is exactly what they did.

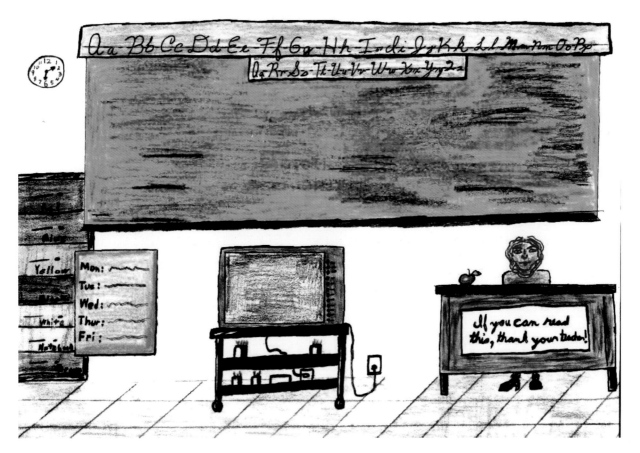

My Classroom

By Ciera Jones

My class is the best class ever. My class is the best because we learn lots of things. We learn how to write in cursive. I like this class because we have a big brown television set. I also like this class because we have a schedule.

This class has different kinds of paper. Mostly, we have overhead paper. We also have construction paper and notebook paper. We have all kinds of things in this class.

This class has a colorful shelf for our writing. The first color on the shelf is red. The second color on the shelf is blue. The last color on the shelf is brown. Our shelf is as colorful as can be.

We have a cart full of school supplies in our class. Red pens are one of the supplies on the cart. There are also red pencils and a pack of 70 envelopes on the cart.

We have lots of supplies in this class.

The Cat

By Ashley Cunningham

Once upon a time, there was a cat. It was a girl cat. Her name was Ashley. She lived with an old fisherman and his wife. They had a daughter named Jessica.

Jessica liked cats. The cat was black with a white furry tail. Sometimes, the cat liked to rub on Jessica's leg when it was hungry. The cat ate many different things. It ate bugs and many other things.

The cat liked to play with people, like Jason. It came to everybody. The cat was kind of fat. Ashley always came to Jessica because she was its mom.

Easter Time

By Kanisha Marsha Hugue

My cousin and I always gather eggs for Easter. We set up a parents' hunt. We all boil eggs. I'm the cook. After that, we all make designs and dye them.

My cousins, Melania and Bush, dye and dry the eggs. Then they hide them.

I like it on Easter. We celebrate and have fun. We all sing songs. When all of the family gets there, we will dance.

A Walk in the Woods

By Chelsea Harrell

If I could be a special buddy to a new student in my neighborhood, I would show her what makes our community unique. I would take her on a walk in the mountains.

At first glance, the mountains may just look like trees and plants. I would show her how to look more closely, and to see not just a simple tree, but also, the brown tree snake clinging to a branch.

We walk further into the woods listening to the sounds getting stronger. All of a sudden, we find ourselves in the midde of a party with shining crystal balls of dew sparkling in the morning sun. Birds sing and butterflies sway gracefully in the wind like dancers. When the dew is gone and the birds start to fly away to search for food, we go looking for more action.

As we walk, we hear squirrels chattering about our presence in the forest. Suddenly startled, a raccoon family jumps up into some trees. They chatter alarmingly.

As we walk toward a low hill, we duck behind a big rock. Just on the other side of the rock is a mother bear with three cubs. We don't want to disturb them, so we are very quiet as we slink away.

Thinking about the animals we have encountered as we go trotting back home, I hope my buddy has enjoyed our walk as much as I.

A Very Strange Tiger

By Preston Carwile

There was a tiger who said, "HELLO!"
He was a very funny fellow.
He tried to climb a tree,
But instead, he drank some tea.
On his break, he liked to eat Jello,
And then, draw a picture
OF Y-E-L-L-O-W.

Drumming For Freedom

By Lindsey Rose Yingst

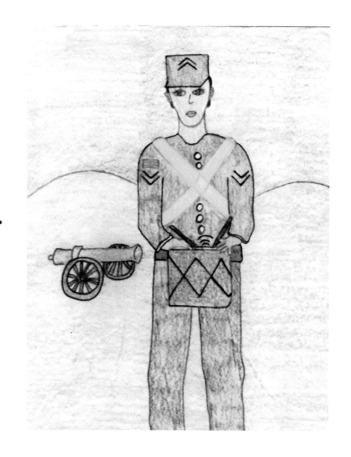

Hi! I am Johnny. I heard the country is divided and the Civil War has started. I will see if I can register to fight.

I am only ten, but I claimed I was 13. That seemed old enough to fight to me, but the official said, "OK, Sonny, you can be a drummer boy. What is your name?"

"Johnny. John R. Fordson."

Father and Mother must be worried about me. Even my five sisters are worried. Especially little Olivia, my youngest sister. When I announced I was joining the Army, Karrie, Laura, Mary, and Netta pouted. But Olivia did not. She wanted to know what an army was. When she heard, she cried for hours and could not be consoled. She clung to me. How I miss little Olivia! Karrie, Laura, and Mary, too. And I guess, Netta, though she snoops a lot, and can read.

The sergeant sent me to an army training camp and they taught me to play the drum. I was disappointed because I thought I would be unimportant in the war. I imagined I'd be couped up inside, while a war was raging on the outside.

Was I ever wrong! I was foolish to join the army. I am obliged to go and play the drum right smack in the middle of the battle. Many a time I've been shot at.

I have some friends that are ten and eleven who also lied about their age. We do not sleep at night. We gamble. So far, I have five dollars and a watch. I will give Karrie, Laura, Mary, Netta and myself a dollar. Since Olivia is my favorite, I'll give her the watch. One of my friends, Vaughn, got lucky once and won a chicken to eat.

After a battle is over, I pick up dead bodies. The cold skin feels eerie on mine. I have seen too much death and blood, for a boy of ten. I suppose it would be worse if I was fighting. I wish this cruel war was over.

I hear the sergeant shouting something.

"What? What sergeant?" I ask.

"This is the last battle. If we win, the war is over!"

I hope we win. I hope I don't die. Please! Let me be a credit to Father, Mother, Karrie, Laura, Mary, Netta, and Olivia. Please let us win, for slavery is wrong and cruel.

The battle starts. I drum as hard and loud as possible, hoping to encourage the soldiers. It does. They fight hard. I watch Lokie, a drummer boy, die. I run over and hold his hand. Lokie yells for his mother, and then dies.

Soon, the General surrenders. He had less than 300 men left. I was joyful. I hugged Vaughn. Then, I hugged the General. He seemed surprised. One of the soldiers got his gun to shoot me, but the General said, "No. Leave him alone!"

I started walking home. After three days, I got there. Mother was weeding the garden. "Ma!" I said, my voice shaking. Mother turned around, a look of pure disbelief on her face. I ran into her arms, crying. Mother stroked my hair. Father came up. He hugged me, too, and told me how proud he was. Karrie, Laura, Mary, Netta, and Olivia came out, too. They hugged me, especially little Olivia. I distributed the gifts, kissed each head, and hugged each little body. I hugged Olivia the longest. It's good to be home.

Slavery is over. Our country is united again. Hopefully, our country will never be divided again.

I Hear The Bells
By Devarus Moore

I
hear the bells
ringing in my heart.
In my heart, they
ring in a beautiful way.
They sing in a harmonizing
way. Ding-dong, Ding-dong.
The bells sing a song in a slow and
noisy way. They sing that song, that
peaceful
song.
I
hear
it
every-
day.

Rats, Cats, and Shrinking Humans

By Seth Rushton

I was so mad! My dad, Jake Lorin, was making me stay at his office after school. My dad is a biochemist, so I figured all I'd see is a couple of nerds.

"If you will be nice and don't mess with anything, I'll take you to Chucky Cheeses," said my father.

"Dad, I'm not six years old anymore, I am twelve.

"I know, but Jacob, you've still got to behave," said Dad.

"Whatever", I said, and walked off.

"I'm ready for the weekend," I sang as I came out of school on Friday afternoon. "I am cool, I'm awesome, I'm... going to my dad's office," I said as I suddenly remembered that I was going to spend two hours at dad's office. Right then my dad pulled into the driveway.

"C'mon, my little pirate," my dad called out in front of all my friends. They all burst out laughing at me! I pretended that I didn't know him. "C'mon," Dad said.

I still ignored him. "Oh Jakie Wakie, Jakeman, Jake Ja Ja..." My dad went down the list of all the names he called me when I was four!!!

"Fine," I said, "Will you just hush!!"

Off we drove.

"Now stay right there and don't move," my dad instructed.

"Yeah, yeah," I said. "Listen Dad, just because I accidentally dropped a bottle of Ionize acid and started a fire doesn't mean that I'm stupid." He looked at me for a few seconds.

"Okay, I'll be off now. Don't touch stuff," my dad said. My dad walked out and closed the door. RESTRICTED AREA, RADIATION INSIDE

"Show time," I shouted. I walked around and found the door. On the door was a sticker that said RESTRICTED AREA, RADIATION INSIDE."

"Ooh, I'm scared," I said in a whimpy voice. I opened the door and went inside. I saw lots of strange bottles.

"The deadly experiments of Dr. Freak," I said in a strange voice. "Ooh, what's this?" I asked myself in the voice. "It's a shampoo!" I said pouring it on me. Then I saw the label on the empty bottle. It said "miniaturization."

"Uh! Oh!" I said. All of a sudden my shoes grew, or so it seemed. Actually, I was shrinking!! I felt myself shrinking. I got smaller and smaller. My shirt and pants got doused with the stuff too, so they shrank with me. I stopped shrinking when I was about four inches tall. This was not my day, because right then a cat strolled in!

"Gee Willikers!" I yelled as the cat spotted me. The cat bounced at me. I saw my escape, a mouse hole. I jumped and the cat landed inches behind me! I was centimeters from the hole, when I felt a paw grab my foot. I was trapped! "Help! Someone help me!" I yelled.

I then heard a squeaky "Yeha". A toothpick flew by me and struck the cat in the paw.

"Yeow!" the cat roared. He dropped me and I saw the mouse with a catapult. I bolted for the mouse hole.

"Aye, ye scurvy lookin mouse," the mouse said. "We been

wondering if ye want to help us in our war?"

"Uh ...I'll pass." The mice were in a war with the giant rats. "Ye could help us aye bundle," he said. "Oye know what will make you want to join us. The cats used to be as small as us, but they went off an got and en-larger machine. Got bigger they did."

"So what's the point?" I asked.

"With the enlarger machine, you can return to your normal size."

"My normal size!" I shouted. "Sure!"

The next day, I was a crew member on the USS Cheese. Our mission was to capture the cat's ship Miss Fast Food! They had the enlarger machine on board.

All of a sudden, the boat rocked! I looked to my left and saw the Miss Fast Food! They had fired a giant pebble at us.

"Arm the cannons!" yelled Capt. Pyro. I got to a cannon, loaded the cannon ball, loaded the gun powder, stuffed it all together, then pulled the rope.

Pooooooooow! Bang!!!! My cannon ball hit their forward cannon allowing us to board the ship. I drew my sword, and went on board. "CLING, CLANG!" There was a battle all around me.

I ran into the captain's room. There on the floor was the enlarger machine! I pushed a button on it and I started to grow! When I was full size, I helped the mice destroy the Miss Fast Food.

I went home that night and fell asleep pronto. It had been a long two days!!

KEISHA'S FIRST DAY AT SCHOOL
By Ongela N. Hill

There was once a little girl name Keisha. She lived in Greenwood with her mother and brother. They had lived in Greenwood for nine years. One day, Keisha's mother told her that they were going to move because she had gotten another job. They were going to move to a little town named Plum Branch.

The first thing that Keisha and her brother Emanuel wanted to know was, if Plum Branch had a mall. When Keisha and her family moved to Plum Branch she really liked it, even though they didn't have a shopping mall or many stores.

As the days drew closer for school to begin, Keisha was beginning to get very nervous with the idea of starting a new school.

The next day Keisha's mother got up very early to go to register the kids for school. Keisha stayed at home and played with the next door neighbor's child. Keisha's mother asked if she wanted to go with her and take a look at the school, but Keisha said that she would rather stay home and play with Marissa.

The first day of school finally arrived. When Keisha arrived at McCormick Elementary School, she was excited because she was going to be in the fourth grade and this would be the first year that she would be changing classes. Her teachers were Mrs. Stirling, Mrs. Creswell, Mrs. Brown, Mrs. Rucker, and Mrs. Kissell. The teachers were very nice. The principal, Mrs. Brown, welcomed Keisha and her mother to the school.

In each class, Keisha made a new friend. Their names were Alfredneka, Savannah, Evelyn, and Pentrae. Keisha was very shy because she was the new kid at school. Keisha did not think that she would fit in with the other kids. She did not think she was a smart as the other kids in her class. The kids tried including Keisha in their games and other fun activities, but Keisha just didn't seem to be able to or fit in.

After school was over, Keisha met her brother at the bus stop to go home. He was very excited about his first day of school. However, Keisha was not as excited. When he asked her, "How did your day go?" she just said, "I don't want to talk about it." Her brother told her that maybe she was just having a hard time because she missed her old school and her old friends. He also told Keisha that she would have to give it some time and then it would be okay.

When Keisha and her brother got home from school, their mom was waiting for them with snacks. She started to tell them about her first day on her new job. "Everyone was very nice and I think I'm going to really like working here," she said.

And before she could ask Emanuel about his day, he blurted out exuberantly how his day went. "I met all kinds of people, and the extra activities are out of sight."

"Oh, I'm so happy to hear that you had a great day," said the mother. Then she looked over at Keisha expecting to hear the same good news, but Keisha just said softly, "Everyone was nice." She just didn't think that anyone really liked her and she didn't think that she would ever fit in. Keisha's mother asked if anyone had said or done anything to her to make her feel that way. Keisha said, "No."

Her mother told her the same thing that her brother had said, "Maybe you are having such a hard time because you just miss the old school and your old friends". Her mother told her to just give it some time and that tomorrow was a new day.

After dinner, Keisha and Emanuel watched TV for a while. Then it was time for bed. Their mother told them to go straight upstairs and brush their teeth. Keisha asked her mother if she would tell her a bedtime story. Her mother told her that she would come and tell her a story after she finished brushing her teeth. Keisha said, "Okay," and rushed off to the bathroom. Keisha's mother sat down on the side of her bed. She said wisely, "Instead of reading one of the books from the shelf tonight, Keisha, I think I'll tell you this story that's not in a book." She began to tell the story about another little girl whose family moved from one town to another and how hard it was for this little girl to adjust to her new school. She told her that it was hard for her to make new friends. She also told her that no matter how hard this little girl tried to make friends or no matter how nice everyone treated her, she just didn't seem to fit in.

102

The reason she had such a hard time was, just like you, she really missed her old school and her old friends. By the time Keisha's mother had gotten to the middle of the story, Keisha had fallen asleep. While Keisha was sleeping she began to dream that she was at school and her friends were trying to get her to play a game. At first, Keisha was afraid. Then she decided to give the game a try.

When Keisha woke up the next morning, she was very excited about going to school and she could not wait to talk to her mother about the story she had told her the night before. Keisha was so excited that she could hardly get dressed. She was the first person down stairs that morning.

When her mother and Emanuel came into the kitchen, Keisha was eating a bowl of cereal. Her mother was very surprised to see that she wasn't nervous or afraid to go to school as she had been before. She asked Keisha what had happened to make her change her mind about school. Keisha told her mother about her dream. She also told her the bedtime story helped her, too. She said that she was not afraid to go to school anymore.

Keisha's mother said, "I'm glad to see you so happy about school." Their mother also told them that they needed to finish their breakfast because the bus would be coming soon. Keisha looked up at her mother and said, "I have just one more question, Mom."

"What is it sweetie?" she asked. "That bedtime story you told me last night, was that little girl you?"

Keisha's mother smiled and said, "Yes, I was that little girl in the story."

Keisha smiled back and said, "I love you Mom."

I Am The Ocean

By: Ryan Cooper, Charlie Diez, Renauta Jack,
Isida Konda, Nikolas Meadows

I am the ocean,
Wide and deep,
Currents glide through me,
So I never sleep.

I am the ocean,
So come and know,
How eons ago,
I shaped this earth,
With my joyous birth.
I am the ocean,
Slowly, slowly.
By the hour,
I re-form the land,
With my great power,
I am the ocean,
With pools of green and silent blue,
I offer up my song to you.
I am the place,
Where the rivers meet the sea,
Swiftly flowing into me.
I am the ocean,
The birds pierce my watery flesh,
To bring fish back to their high up nest.
I am the ocean,
As the rain falls into me,
A rainbow forms to meet my sea.
I am the ocean,
A gentle giant jumps into the air,
Thrashing furiously without a care.

I am the ocean,
As twilight falls upon the sea,
People look out comforting me.

Catch a Wave to the Beach

By: Lisa VanBuskirk, Holly Gray, Jaime Chapman

It was the day of the big event. We were going on a field trip to the beach. It was going to be great. I was just getting off the bus, and it felt good to feel the warm, gritty sand under my feet. Our class got to have a picnic, then we went swimming. At least some of us went swimming. I didn't know how, but thank goodness, no one knew.

After swimming, we had our picnic; and when we were all done eating, Katie called over to me, "Trey, want to go swimming?"

I responded, "No, I just ate. Maybe later, though." Thank goodness, I got out of it that time, but I didn't know what I'd do about it later.

The air was crisp, and it felt good. Our class had come to the beach because we were studying oceanic life. The teacher was jabbering on as usual about the ocean like it was the most important thing in the world. I didn't care much about the ocean except that it was water, and I couldn't swim. Katie was walking toward me. My mind started racing. I knew she would ask me to go swimming with them. "Hey, Trey," yelled Katie.

"What?"

"Do you want to go swimming now?"

"Um, I forgot my bathing suit."

"Trey, you're wearing your suit."

"Oh, yeah. I guess I forgot."

"Well, it's lots of fun out there. Come join us."

"Okay, maybe later," I said.

In just a short while, I heard Mrs. Nabisco holler, "Come on, kids! It's time to go. The bus is pulling out."

"Oh, no," I thought. Katie and Abbie are still in the water. They can't hear the teacher.

I went to the edge of the water and called, "Katie, Abbie. Come on. It's time to go."

I heard my friends call back, "We can't. We can't get back in."

"Great," I thought. "Now I have no choice but to go in and get them. If I don't, they'll drown; and I'll never forgive myself." I started running into the water. "What am I doing?" I asked myself. "I can't swim." Still, I didn't stop. Now I was in the water waist deep, and I could see my friends thrashing about in the water, bobbing up and down. I tried to get to them. Finally, I reached them and pulled them from under the blanket of swirling water.

I dragged them up on the beach, and they started coughing. Abbie and Katie looked at me through their water-logged eyes. "Thank you," they said.

"You're welcome," I said joyfully. "And thank you!"

They looked at me like I was out of my mind. Maybe they would never know why I was thanking them, but it wasn't important for them to know.

We walked slowly together to the bus. All three of us were thankful for the experience. It was a field trip we wouldn't soon forget.

The Wolf and the Chicken

By: Brigette Evans

There once were two best friends - a wolf and a chicken. One day the wolf invited the chicken over to dinner. Without thinking, she said, "Yes." She arrived at the wolf's house. He opened the door. "Step in," he said. When they were settled, he asked, "What would you like to have?" "Worms," she said. Then she asked him, "What do you want?" He turned around with a grin. He said, "I want fried chicken." The wolf cooked the chicken, and had fried chicken.

MORAL: THINK BEFORE SAYING YES TO SOMEONE.

Two Best Friends

By: Amber Peak, Leandra Smith,
Joshua Trapp and Brian Watkins

Once there were two dogs. They were best friends. One day, they both had puppies and were proud fathers. One dog was jealous of the other dogs puppy. The next day, one of the dogs stole the other dogs puppy. The other dog soon found out who stole his puppy. He got his puppy and they were never friends again.
MORAL: NEVER STEAL FROM SOMEONE ELSE.

Kiramak

By: Amber Peak

Once there was the most beautiful flower in the world. Its name was Kiramak. There was only one Kiramak left in the world. Fall came and it bloomed. It finally was about to release its seedlings, when a boy came and picked it. This boy was a scientist and knew about the Kiramak flower. He was just about to put it in a pot, when he noticed there were no roots. It soon died.

There were no more Kiramak flowers.

MORAL: NEVER HARM ANY PART OF NATURE, BECAUSE SOME THINGS CAN NOT BE REPLACED.

The Student Who Didn't Listen

By: Jeremy Shannon

There once was a boy, who had a test on Monday. It was Saturday. He remembered that the teacher said, "Study over the weekend." He didn't study the whole weekend. He played baseball, basketball, and football on Saturday. He went to church on Sunday.

It was time to get up for school on Monday. He got ready for school. He rode with his mom. The boy went into the gym. He walked to the classroom. The day went by quickly. It was the end of the day. The teacher passed out the test. He was the first one finished. He got an F-. When he got home his mom got mad because of his grade.

MORAL: ALWAYS FOLLOW DIRECTIONS.

The Elephant and The Rat

By: Titiahna Belton, Kelsey McDonald, Brigette Evans
Deandre Robinson and Jonathon Yarborough

This fable is about an elephant named Brandon, a rat named Brigette, and a red tail hawk named Titiahna. Brandon and Brigette were best friends, until one day, Brandon stepped on Brigette's tail. Jonathon, a bee, was flying by. He did not like what he saw. Jonathon stung Brandon. After Jonathon stung Brandon, Titiahna tried to eat Jonathon, but Brigette saved Jonathon.

MORAL: DON'T BE FRIENDS WITH AN ENEMY.

Tony and Tom

By: Kelsey McDonald

Once there was a duck named Tony, and a frog named Tom. One day, Tony and Tom decided to dig a hole through the earth so they could go to China. They started to dig. After two days, they had dug all the way to China. In China they met five people. The people spoke different in China. Tony said,Tom I know some Chinese talk. The next day, Tony and Tom could not find their hole. So, they lived with the Chinese people and they lived happily ever after.

MORAL: NEVER MAKE A DECISION UNLESS YOU ARE SURE ABOUT IT.

Wolf and Fox

By: Timothy Brooks Smith

One day, a wolf and fox were playing in their field with woods beside it, and they stopped playing. The fox said, "Why did we stop playing?"

The wolf said, "Let's make a bet."

The fox said, "Okay. What is the bet?"

Then the wolf said, "The bet is I can stay in the woods for one night."

The fox said, "Don't do it. It is dangerous, you could get hurt."

The wolf said, "I won't get hurt!"

Finally, it was night and the wolf and the fox went into the woods. The wolf went in and laid down. He fell asleep. Then he heard a growl and woke up. It was a big growl like a bear's. It was a bear. "Aaahhh," said the wolf. He got up and ran and ran. He was out of the woods and the bear didn't catch him.

MORAL: DON'T DO SOMETHING THAT IS
DANGEROUS. YOU MIGHT GET HURT.

John

By: Brittany Orr, Jeremy Shannon and
Timothy Brooks Smith

One day, a boy named John asked his mother if he could go play outside with his friend Joseph. She said, "Yes, just as long as you don't play in the street." After a while, Joseph decided that he would throw a hard throw. He threw the ball into the street. John went to get the ball. A red Firebird was coming. It got closer until it ran over the ball. The car made the ball bounce.

It hit John in the head and knocked him down. Joseph started running into the street. An older man got there first. Joseph ran into the house to get John's mother. They both came running into the street. John's mother accused the man of hitting her child.

MORAL: DONT ACCUSE SOMEONE OF DOING SOMETHING UNLESS YOU SAW THEM DO IT.

The Bird and The Cat

By: Leandra Smith

One day, there was a bird sitting in a tree. He started crowing, and a cat heard him. The cat quickly ran over to the tree, ran up the tree, and tried to eat the bird. The bird flew away. The next day, a dog saw the cat and ran after him. The cat asked the bird to help him, but he didn't, and the dog ate the cat.

MORAL: DON'T BOTHER ANYONE BECAUSE THEY MAY NOT HELP YOU WHEN YOU NEED HELP.

The Dragon
By
Leandra
Smith

There were two boys. Their names were Colin and Keenan. They lived in China. One day, the boys decided to go swimming in the Old River. As they walked towards the river, an old Chinese man stopped them. He said, "Don't get into the river, you will get eaten by the large dragon!" The boys played and paid no attention to the old man. They said, "Sit down you wrinkled man." And they ran in the river. A few minutes passed as they were in the water. Keenan noticed something in the water. It was the dragon. The dragon stood up and ate them both in one gulp.

MORAL: LISTEN TO OLDER PEOPLE.

The Fearless Squirrel and Fearful Bobcat

By: Shane Martin

Once upon a time, there was a fearful bobcat and a little fearless squirrel. One day, the bobcat saw the little squirrel. The squirrel ran one way and the bobcat ran the other way. Then the squirrel looked back, and the squirrel saw the bobcat running the other way. The squirrel turned around and caught up with the bobcat, and told the bobcat, "I should be the prey and you should be the predator."

The bobcat said, "I am just a fearful bobcat." "Well, this is your lucky day."

"I am going to teach you how to not be scared of everything. Let's go to the fields," said the squirrel.

"I am going to teach you how to be a real bobcat." The squirrel taught the bobcat how to catch a prey. Then, when the bobcat saw the squirrel, the squirrel became the bobcat's prey.

MORAL: LITTLE ANIMALS CAN SOMETIMES TEACH BIG ANIMALS LESSONS, BUT NEVER HELP YOUR ENEMY.

Ugly and Pretty

By: Tatiahna Belton

There once was a lady who lived in China. Her name was Lin Su. She was a poor lady and didn't have very much. Everyone in the town thought she was an ugly lady, but they did not say that to her face. There was also a lady who lived in Ohio. Her American name was Nicole. She was a very pretty lady. She could get anyone to do anything for her. But, she had to move to China because the law found out that she had crossed the boundary without them knowing her real name was Kin Lu.

When she went back to China, the people in China had prepared a special dinner for her. Everyone in the town came. When they saw Lin Su, they all whispered to each other and started laughing at her. But, she did not care about it. When Kin Lu saw her, she went to the front of the room and said, "That is one ugly lady there."

Lin Su said, "My child you will be sorry you said that." The next day when Kin Lu woke up, her teeth and hair had fallen out, but Lin Su was beautiful again.

MORAL: DON'T PICK AT SOMEONE WHO DRESSES BADLY OR LOOKS WORSE THAN YOU DO.

Best Friends

By: Brittany Orr

There once was a Rottweiler named Rocky. He had a friend named Snoopy. He was a Doberman Pinscher. They were best friends until a new dog came into the neighborhood named PeeWee. He was a German Shepherd.

One day, Snoopy and PeeWee were playing. They hadn't played with Rocky for about a week and a half. So, Rocky was getting curious. The next day, Rocky went walking. He saw Snoopy and PeeWee having a good old time. Rocky got mad. After that, Rocky started playing and hanging with his bigger brother.

MORAL: NEVER GIVE UP YOUR BEST FRIEND FOR
        SOMEONE NEW.

The Monkeys and The Goat

By: Russell Branham,
Cha-won Hall,
and
Yolanda Young

There once lived three rich and lazy monkeys, but they had one problem. They found out they had hired a lazy servant. They called him Lazy Goat. Then one day, they decided to go out and find a female servant to help Lazy Goat. Her name was Penny the Goat. She was very attractive and always attended to her work.

The Lazy Goat thought the monkeys were trying to teach him a lesson. He got the point, got off his duff and went to work. And, he was never called Lazy Goat again.

MORAL: LAZINESS GET'S YOU NOWHERE.

HOMONYMS

write

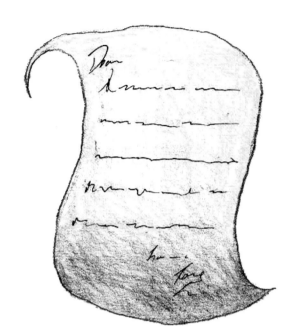

This is the *write* when you

right

This is the *right* like left and

hair

My sis-
ter has
a lot of
hair.

hare

I saw a
hare in
my
back
yard.

ate

I _ate_
two
pieces
of pizza.

eight

The
number
eight.

hear 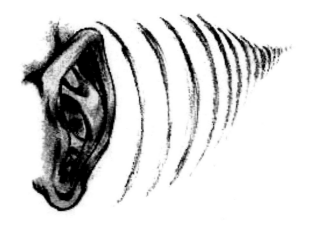 I can
hear.

here  Come
here
please.

122

mail  The Mail Lady puts the *mail* in the mail box.

male  My dad and I are *males*.

dear

Use *dear* when you write to people.

deer

This is the animal *deer*.

eye   **I have two _eyes_.**

I  **_I_ am a person.**

Don't Bug
By Arlene Perez

Don't bug me!
I said don't bug me!
Don't bug me or eeelllsssseee!!!
Don't bug me, I mean it!
SPLAT!
I said, don't bug me.

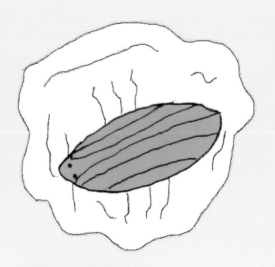

Ewww!!!
Bug juice.

126

Fleas

By Chelsea Walsh

Fleas on my dog,
Fleas on my cat,
Fleas on my rabbit,
So how about that?

I can't help it,
If I scratch.
They're sooooo annoying.

Fleas,
Please don't hatch!

Bees

By Courtney Scott

I went outside,
I saw a bee,
He gave me
An unpleasant sting.

I said,
What's wrong with you,
Stupid bee?
Nobody ever stings me.

I'm going to count to
Three,
And you'd better be gone,
Stupid bee.

FRIENDS
By Allysa Woods

FRIENDS ARE SPECIAL PEOPLE.
THEY ARE PEOPLE YOU CAN COUNT ON.

WHEN YOU'RE TOGETHER,
YOU CAN CHEER EACH OTHER AND
YOU CAN TALK TO EACH OTHER
WHEN YOU ARE SAD.
THAT'S WHAT FRIENDS ARE FOR.

THE MAIN THING,
IS TO BE AROUND EACH OTHER.
FRIENDS, FRIENDS, FRIENDS,
THEY'RE ALWAYS THERE.
THAT'S WHAT FRIENDS ARE FOR.

Supporters and Sponsors

J.L. SCOTT REALTY CO., INC
SOUTH CAROLINA INTERNATIONAL READERS ASSOCIATION
CLAFLIN COLLEGE, ART DEPT., HERMAN KEITH, CHAIRMAN
RADIO, PRINT & TELEVISION MEDIA
DISTRICT SUPERINTENDENTS
BLUE CROSS & BLUE SHIELD
SC POULTRY FEDERATION
INTERNATIONAL PAPER
JOHNNY PRINGLE
CHEM-NUCLEAR
RICHARD DAVIS
VERNA MOORE
NATIONS BANK
BELL SOUTH
WAL-MART
C P & L
SCANA
A T&T
COCA-COLA CONSOLIDATED,
BRYANT SUMTER AND KELVIN GADSEN

GOVERNOR, JIM HODGES
SOUTH CAROLINA GENERAL ASSEMBLY
SPEAKER OF THE HOUSE, DAVID WILKINS
SEN. YANCEY MCGILL
SCDOT, ELIZABETH S. MABRY
SC DEPT OF PUBLIC SAFETY, B. BOYKIN ROSE
MUNICIPAL ASSOCIATION OF SOUTH CAROLINA
SC CONFERENCE OF BLACK MAYORS ASSOCIATION
SOUTH CAROLINA EDUCATION ASSOCIATION
SC LEGISLATIVE BLACK CAUCUS, SEN. JOHN MATTHEWS
STATE SUPERINTENDENT OF EDUCATION, INEZ TENENBAUM
LT. GOVERNOR, BOB PEELER

MAYESVILLE EDUCATIONAL AND INDUSTRIAL INSTITUTE,
W.M. JEFFERSON, PRESIDENT

First Annual Dr. Bethune Children Author's Book Fair
List of Judges

Shanai Harris	WIS TV, Anchor - Columbia, SC
Ellen Parson	Director of Student Media, University of South Carolina, Columbia, SC
Joan C. Scott	Promotion & Marketing, Columbia, SC
Carol Shough	Author, Columbia, SC
Jane Dyke	Professional Librarian, Midland Elementary School North Charleston, SC
Dan Stevenson	Linguist, Winnsboro, SC
Helen Fellers	Community Relations Coordinator Barnes & Noble, Richland Mall
Willette Stocker	WQMC, Sumter, SC
L. Zimmerman-Keitt	Claflin College, Project Life, Orangeburg, SC
Katherine Price	Communications Coordinator, The State Newspaper Columbia, SC
Ron Anderson	State Library for the Blind and Handicapped, Columbia, SC
Katrina Lehman	Community Relations Coordinator, Barnes & Noble, Greenville, SC

*Like running in
the big race,
writing is
"one step at a time."*